THIS IS ME! 2022

VOICES OF THE FUTURE

Edited By Daisy Job

First published in Great Britain in 2022 by:

Young Writers
Remus House
Coltsfoot Drive
Peterborough
PE2 9BF
Telephone: 01733 890066
Website: www.youngwriters.co.uk

All Rights Reserved
Book Design by Ashley Janson
© Copyright Contributors 2022
Softback ISBN 978-1-83928-990-3

Printed and bound in the UK by BookPrintingUK
Website: www.bookprintinguk.com
YB0521A

FOREWORD

For Young Writers' latest competition This Is Me, we asked primary school pupils to look inside themselves, to think about what makes them unique, and then write a poem about it! They rose to the challenge magnificently and the result is this fantastic collection of poems in a variety of poetic styles.

Here at Young Writers our aim is to encourage creativity in children and to inspire a love of the written word, so it's great to get such an amazing response, with some absolutely fantastic poems. It's important for children to focus on and celebrate themselves and this competition allowed them to write freely and honestly, celebrating what makes them great, expressing their hopes and fears, or simply writing about their favourite things. This Is Me gave them the power of words. The result is a collection of inspirational and moving poems that also showcase their creativity and writing ability.

I'd like to congratulate all the young poets in this anthology, I hope this inspires them to continue with their creative writing.

CONTENTS

Independent Entries

Sohayb El Hana (10)	1
Ella Scott (10)	2
Jennifer Lewis (11)	4
Mia Zolotova (9)	7
Violet O'Brien-Perry (10)	8
Arnav Ghoshal (10)	10
Fatima Noor (10)	13
Shiyam Thulasiraj (8)	14
Ethan Theo Gao (10)	16
Alfie Sandford (9)	18
Carter Austin Curran (9)	20
Daisy Clarke (9)	22
Amal Furaji (11)	24
Elodie Penhale (9)	26
Essylve Kakesa (10)	28
Safia Yazdani (11)	30
Prethivee Ananth (9)	32
Molly Raybould (9)	34
Varunikka Muraleekumar (10)	36
Elowen Doidge (9)	38
Aisha Yusuf (10)	40
Nathan Smith (9)	42
Katie Hamilton (10)	44
Vaanika Sahajpal	46
Bradley Bowers (8)	48
Savannah Javed (11)	50
Kaycie Bradbury (9)	51
Réiko McDonald (10)	52
Aneel Kaur Kooner (9)	54
Hope Boyle (9)	55
Mia Godfrey (9)	56
Scarlett Milbourne (10)	58
Hannah McMurray (9)	60
Liam O'Connor (11)	62
Zelphi Fine Naidu (11)	63
Navleen Kaur	64
Isabella Nikolov (8)	65
Erika Middleton (9)	66
Jasmin Sehdev (9)	67
Bhargavi Rajanikanth (10)	68
Nyma Jawwad (11)	70
Georgia-Mae Smith (10)	71
Sophia Piper (10)	72
Janna Oyedeji (9)	74
Aradhya Adeesh (9)	76
Faith Umeadi (11)	78
Oyinlola Fadairo (9)	80
Hoda Ahmed (11)	82
Olivia Marsh (7)	84
Isabelle Jordan (9)	86
Amelia Curley (9)	88
Millie Guyll-Wiggins (11)	89
Grace Boyle (7)	90
Phoebe Stanford (10)	91
Lila Barasi (10)	92
Lianne Bnouni (11)	93
Azhahinii Ravishankar (9)	94
Esme Yates	96
Mimi Tian (8)	98
Ava Swift (10)	100
Kaiyah-Rayne Garratt (10)	101
Aaiesha Mohamed Faizal (10)	102
Anna Wieckiewicz (10)	103
Christopher Regha (8)	104
Akshitha Arun Prasanth (8)	106
Isaac De Vilder (11)	107
Finnlay Annetts (9)	108
Aaron Skandarajah-Vazquez (8)	109
Skyla Washington (11)	110

Name	No.
Connie Allen (11)	112
Anaya Smart (9)	113
William Bolton (10)	114
Thomas Moore (10)	116
Charlie Dimelow (9)	117
Maria Miah (10)	118
Regina Jalloh	119
Thomas Whitting	120
Milo Pollard (9)	122
Zofia Lewandowska (10)	123
Lucy Pankhurst (8)	124
Elliot Newman (8)	125
Jemima Clifford (9)	126
Kaaviniyal Ilanthendral (9)	127
Anaya Khan (9)	128
Seren Grace Joy-Rooney (9)	129
John Griffiths (8)	130
Josie Day (11)	131
Alfie Summerfield (8)	132
Anjayen Ananda (10)	133
Zoya Iqbal (9)	134
Isla Aitken (9)	135
Arsh Khan (10)	136
Yousef Aburadi	137
Daniel Moore (11)	138
Sky Kwok (8)	139
Eva Wright (8)	140
Seren Smart (11)	141
Oliver Cross-Monaghan (10)	142
Josh Townsend	143
Fareed Ahmed (8)	144
Ayden Panesar (10)	145
Zahra Miah (8)	146
Alfie Donnelly (9)	147
Olivia Lauffer	148
Omar Faisal (7)	149
Ellis Edwards (7)	150
Avni Saraswathi (8)	151
Michael Neeman (10)	152
Kavithan Davidprapakaran (8)	153
Kai Hendricks Bryant	154
Binyamin Bhamji (9)	155
Liza Hussain	156
Himavarsha Manchikanti (9)	157
Dylan Gill (11)	158
Jasper Cashman (9)	159
Henry Miller (9)	160
Kai Runaghan	161
Ruiwen Gong (8)	162
Nathan Moore (10)	163
Tanvi Saraswathi (8)	164
Hiba Ahmed (6)	165
Samuel Menakaya (10)	166
Brandon Ford (10)	167
Isabella Ritson (8)	168
Jessica Shaw (8)	169
Chloe Lam (10)	170
Alice Walton	171
Riley Randles	172
Emily S (9)	173
Isobel Tombs (9)	174
Madison Sullivan (9)	175
Aania Bhamji (8)	176
Benedict Swift (9)	177

THE POEMS

About Me!

Every day, I open my eyes and my mum gives me a soft hug as warm as a radiator.
As I start my home-schooling day, fun knocks at my door.
Whilst I study, I keep daydreaming about football and my favourite players.

When my family and I enter the heart of the local wood, we hear the huge trees hum in happiness. While in nature, I reflect on how every day I grow like a bud in fertile soil.

So many sports to try when you're a sporty guy!
As I pick up my fencing foil, I am instantly flooded with points.
Once the football hits the net, I feel like I have the World Cup in my hands.

Back home, my stomach rumbling, I open the fridge to find the stench of my mum's camembert pounding me to the floor.

As the sun retreats for the night and the lights are turned off, fear breaks into my pounding heart...

Sohayb El Hana (10)

My Cake

What to make?
What to bake?
I flick through the recipe book and try to decide what to make.
I finally decide,
A cake!
It would be a vanilla sponge cake and there would be a chocolate drizzle over the top,
It would have an icing fondant which would be a sculpture of a girl playing in the mud
And there would be Smarties and sprinkles pouring out the middle!

I get to work immediately,
Following the recipe step by step,
Adding each ingredient extremely carefully.
Then I put the unfinished cake in the oven,
Hoping it would cook perfectly.
I close the oven door with a slam!
I then get out the frying pan,
And start on the chocolate drizzle.
After that, I get out the icing fondant and start making a sculpture of a girl.

That took an awfully long time,
And by the time I had made the little girl,
The cake was done!

I took the cake out the oven and got the Smarties and sprinkles out of the cupboard.
The cake took ages to cool down.
I started to daydream because waiting was monotonous.
When it did,
I cut a hole in the middle and added the Smarties and sprinkles.
Then I put the cake that I had cut back on the top so it would be a surprise.
I added the drizzle, then the girl, lying face down in the mud!

I showed the cake to my family and then I finally cut it into ten slices.
I tasted the cake, it took me to another world,
It was so gooey and crunchy.
The texture was just right.
I can only say one thing,
I am great at baking.

Ella Scott (10)

Proud To Be Me

Hello, my name is Jennifer Lewis,
I am ten years old.
I am like Elsa,
I never feel the cold.

I love the sea,
The big crashing waves.
The beautiful sea animals
That hide in their caves.

I love playing sports,
But not on the golf course.
I will always want to be number one,
Sorry - it's just too much fun!
I know... I'm competitive,
I can't stop, it's repetitive!

I love to play with my friends,
We have too much fun
And it never ends.

I like to make art,
The colours and shapes.
I like to use this
When making my yummy cakes.

I love to be in my safe place,
My room.
Using creams to make
My face healthy and smooth.

I have a great and stylish wardrobe
Wearing the outfits every weekend.
Put the clothes on
And boom, hit send.

I think I am a very kind and considerate person,
I help people as much as I can do.
Doing kind deeds for everyone,
Including you!

I always do my best,
To help all the rest.
I hope you can too,
Even if it is a cow that says moo!

This is my story,
This you see is me.
I hope you can keep up,
And become friends with me!

F-R-I-E-N-D-S,
Also I am a bit clumsy, watch out for the mess!

This is me!

Jennifer Lewis (11)

This Is Me

Hi, I'm Mia, half British half Russian.
I often get told I have a good sense of fashion.
When I was five I moved from Georgia to Eastleigh
And when I joined school I was as happy as can be.
I made some new friends, Mylissa and Mary,
Also the teachers were a bit scary.
Anyway, I had a dream that I was writing
About two tiny toddlers fighting
And then I thought, *that was strange!*
But yet did I know that things would change.
That very next day
I was writing away!
Stories and poems,
Small riddles with big problems.
I won competitions,
It was a metaphorical mission.
Me and my family are very proud,
I even performed in a small crowd.
And now I'm sat here writing a poem,
Hoping to win Mum a jeroboam.

Mia Zolotova (9)

This Is Me

When I was little I always found things hard.
I never knew how to help myself, except from write it all on card.
I couldn't concentrate and I had so much energy,
But I guess that's just me.

It was the first day of school and I was really nervous.
I knew no one there, I felt like I was under the surface.
My tummy felt sick and I had shaking hands.
I took a deep breath and went into land.
I put my bag away, what do I do next?
I guess I just play, what I do best.
A couple of hours later it was home time
And I told mum all about lunchtime.
"I sat next to Darcie and Summer too.
Could you arrange a playdate soon?"

Each day in every lesson,
I was constantly asking, "What was the question?"
As the years went by, I spoke to more and more people,

Until we got to year five and we mixed classes,
what a surprise!
As that year slowly passed I met Anna, Maisie and Elise,
They're so nice and as cool as ice.
They always help me through a time,
Whenever I don't feel fine.

What I have realised is that disabilities are gifts,
don't let that go away.
Be yourself in your own way.
Yes, I have ADHD
But I'm just happy being me!

Violet O'Brien-Perry (10)

My Humble Home And Me

Another chaotic day passes by,
There is never any peace
The noise is extremely high
It's never at ease

I sit in my room
And drink some water
Suddenly, I hear a loud boom
Which is followed by a babyish 'he he, here!'

I pick her up
Like a loving brother
And give her my cup
She's one like no other

I go downstairs
To help with cleaning what we ate
It's as if we eat like bears
It appeared true, looking at the number of plates!

Other than this
I sometimes wonder
What I am going to be
When I grow older

Will I be an artist
And put my work in a painting archive full of pulchritudinous scenes?
Or a beekeeper
And collect honey from hives full of industrious bees?

Will I be an athlete and win an intense race
Or will I be a dancer, and leap and twirl with elegance and grace?

I wish to be successful and free
To be able to live and later relax under the shade of a tree

I want to spend time with my family
That is how I want to live life happily

Alongside all that,
You must bear in mind that:

Life is full of mysteries
Waiting to unfold
But life is extremely exciting
When you've got it in your hold.

Arnav Ghoshal (10)

The Anger Inside Of Me

Anger lingers behind us all around
It jumps and wiggles, making eerie sounds,
Some hear it while others feel it and can't help but reveal it,
We mope and lope until we squeal, that's how most of us feel,
We're sad and bad, and sometimes mad,
I agree with that because that's sometimes me,
When I'm angry I go red like a chilli and do something silly,
I jump and thump until I scream,
It almost feels like a dream,
I cry and sigh, oh my!
I go to bed, feeling the comforting sensation of sleep
Then suddenly anger has flown away,
With a few warm hugs and sweet words
Anger will disappear...
So don't worry and don't be sorry,
Just keep on a big smile while you're happy,
And don't get snappy!

Fatima Noor (10)

Guess Who I Am

Hold it right there, first of all, this is about me.
Now let me tell the whole story.

I have so much fun in my life.
There's a ton of adventures only seen by me.
I do amazing tricks such as magic tricks.
Maybe I'm supposed to?

I like creating things and drawing pictures.
There's uncountable drawings made by me.
My drawings look unique and stunning.
I feel proud of myself!

Whenever I get dreams it's always curious,
Then two seconds later it seems to happen.
Sometimes I do unusual things,
Like sing when I'm sleeping.

I'm a true person,
If I lie I'll learn my lesson not to.
We always have to say the truth.
Honesty is always the best policy!

If anybody hurts me or makes me cry
I'd remember but also ignore it.

Whenever I'm lonely
I want to go outside.
Sometimes I think of a joyful memory
To make me happy.

You all think I'm just a kid who has nothing to do
But one day you will see the talent within me!

Shiyam Thulasiraj (8)

Meeting Uncertainty

I met Uncertainty.
His eyes were compacted with puzzlement.
His face was filled with indecision.
Red marks penetrated his skin.
Checking his surroundings, not sure of what's around him, he was enveloped in a cloak of invisibility.
Head in a whirlwind, unable to make a decision.
Eyes closed tightly as if trying to think.

I followed him.
His walk was more a tiptoe, more a creep.
Down the steps to the town square he went,
And started his descent down the staircase.
On the sound of Uncertainty I followed,
I saw the tap flowing, and spied him.
The water stopped and I saw a boy.
Uncertainty stood before me.

He halted at the tap's edge,
As he was approached by a thought.
Uncertainty gazed as he unlocked a memory,

He watched as the thought drifted away,
Up into the night sky,
As it floated further and further away,
I saw it go.
Uncertainty wept as he watched his only thought float away,
Developing a circle of uncertainty around him
An inaccessible circle of uncertainty.

I had seen it all,
Uncertainty had explained it all and now,
No longer uncertain.

Ethan Theo Gao (10)

This Is Me

I am a jolly little chappy
And being 9 years old, I no longer need to wear a nappy.
Some people say I am a bundle of fun
And I am as bright as the summer sun.
As a treat, I like to blow bubble gum,
When it goes pop it is so much fun!
I like gummy bears
And I love going to the fun fairs.
I go on the bumper cars with my friends
And drive them around the bends.
I am known for my frilly curls,
They are loved by all the girls.
And I always blush
When they make such a fuss!
Sometimes, my hair is annoying, it never stops growing.
It's like the garden, needs regular mowing.
I love throwing and catching balls
And climbing up great walls.

I love to dance to the sound of the electric guitar
At home or travelling in the car.
I don't like eggs, especially the yolks,
But I love playing practical jokes.
My friends find me funny and think I'm one of a kind,
They are never far away, they are easy to find.
They accept me for who I am and that's a good sign,
We will be friends until the end of time.

Alfie Sandford (9)

I Am 10 Feet Tall

My name is Carter Austin,
I just turned 9 years old.
I've got a story about me
That I'd like to be told.

I have days when I struggle,
Because I get teased about being small,
I smile along and pretend
The names don't bother me at all.

When really it makes me upset and sad,
And really hurts my feelings.
I just wish I'd grow big and tall
Until I can reach the ceiling.

But my mummy says I shouldn't be sad
Instead, I should hold my head up high,
Because I've a personality that is so big and bright
You can see it from the sky.

She says I'm very loving,
And really rather sweet,
That I'm a little stubborn but a great friend,
A great boy from my head to my feet.

She says I'm kind and funny
And really great at playing football,
I'm passionate, fiery but so caring
Who helps friends when they fall.

So when I think about it again,
I'm not bad or weak because I'm small,
I'm a great son and friend who is lots of fun,
And this makes me 10 feet tall.
This is me!

Carter Austin Curran (9)

My Life Is Like A Bridge

My life is like a bridge
With all its different connections
Life is like a bridge
You can choose your path

There might be a large tree
With poisonous fruit
But that tree will give you shelter
If you come across a storm

Your bridge might be strong
Wobbly or unsure
It is yours and only yours
And varies in everything and more

Across the sides might be a bush
With brambles prickly like a pin
But in the autumn, you can go blackberry picking
And make a sweet, yummy crumble

Is there a troll under your bridge
That haunts you when you're sad?
Just walk and take in the fresh air
I don't let my bridge make me mad

My bridge might be pink
Or when I'm envious, green
My life holds my feelings
I might feel yellow or cream

My life is like a bridge
I'll just let it be
Because life is like a bridge
And this poem describes me

Daisy Clarke (9)

Simply Me

There's a little person in me,
Striding through a void of my misery,
Her passion shaded by shame.
But she says, her head held high, "I will not be tamed."

There's a sweet, sweet music box in me,
Playing the same inviting melody.
The gentle notes bond together to create a utopia of sound,
The perfect harmony.
The essence of calm reminds me to cherish every gift and opportunity...

And to always be kind to everybody.

My courageous soul is an avatar,
Wading through the jungles of success,
Discovering new caves of strength,
And unlocking doors full of exciting possibilities.
Can't you see? It's brilliant to be me!

All of these creations lie inside of me.
Me.
It's marvellous to be me!
I am perfectly imperfect,
I celebrate my success,
Conquer all new challenges that lie ahead,

And have new adventures every day.

I couldn't be happier.
Who am I?
Simply me.

Amal Furaji (11)

Lights, Camera, Action

Lights, camera, action
A mix of excitement and fear.
Practice, scripts and fun
You can feel it coming near.

The show day looms in front of me
Like a troll with a rock-hard club.
Us cast are huddled and fretting,
Reminds me of Mum and her cubs.

My heart thuds hard against my ribs,
The crowd is coming now.
I'm confused - do I want it all to end
When I have to stand and bow?

The teacher calls me, it's my cue
I just really have to be brave.
I'm playing a hero, after all
It's a maiden I'm trying to save.

Soon I feel completely elated,
My worry flies away like a dove.
I act like the fabulous queen of the show
My voice floating up, up above.

When it is the end of the show
We all shout, "*Hooray!*"
We've done our best and it was amazing,
It's a very special day.

Lights, camera, action
A mix of excitement and fear.
Practice, scripts and fun
You can feel it coming near.

Elodie Penhale (9)

This Is Essylve Kakesa

T his is me; this is all about me
H appy boy I always am
I nclusive language is my type of talk
S ecure and safe I feel among my friends

I mpatience is not part of me
S adness is not my cup of tea

E ven though every day is different for everyone
S ome days are good and some days are bad for all of us
S illy face is what I make when I disagree
Y ummy food attracts me more
L ike any ordinary boy except that
V ery rarely I get upset
E veryone is important to me

K nowing my strengths and weaknesses makes me strong
A pologising for my mistakes empowers me
K indness is part of me
E nthusiasm makes my day
S ad news makes me angry and depressed
A ccepting and embracing changes remain my rule.

Essylve Kakesa (10)

Autumn's Arrival

As summer says its last goodbyes,
The new dawn shines through autumn skies.
And as the air fills with autumn cheer,
It's finally announced that autumn is here.

Swirling and twirling in the breeze,
Are brightly coloured autumn leaves,
Floating in the autumn cold,
'Til they land in eruptions of red, brown and gold.

As I gaze at the autumn flowers,
I skip through the light, autumn showers,
A colourful pathway crunching under my feet,
Made of acorns and fallen leaves.

All the people wear scarves and gloves,
Tightly holding the ones they love.
And little kids cry with autumn glee,
Jumping in puddles or piles of leaves.

And as summer says its last goodbyes,
The dusk now fades into autumn skies,
And as the cheer, begins to disappear,
It's finally announced that autumn is here.

Safia Yazdani (11)

This Is Me, Prethivee Ananth

Three years and three friends, always hand in hand,
We were part of an amazing band.
Then the day came when our bond broke,
As I was dragged many miles away, not far from Stoke.

A brand-new school with awesome opportunities,
Remarkable new classmates and a new community.
I tried so hard to make new mates,
But failed so miserably, it seemed to be my fate.

Twenty-nine months went by feeling so disowned,
Heartbreak and emptiness filled me as I played all alone.
Then all of a sudden, I seemed to attract,
Two people who felt the same and came to interact.

Two friends who came to play,
And who never went away.
Just like me, one loves unicorns and Harry Potter,
And the other likes makeup and sport, what a shocker!

Our friendship that has been long-awaited,
I feel so elated,
They like me for who I am,
And not someone else, whose life is all glam,

This is me, silly but timid,
This is me Prethivee Ananth.

Prethivee Ananth (9)

Day

When I wake up in the morning
The first thing I hear is the sound of snoring
I slip into my dressing gown and walk down the stairs
To see my dog covered in hairs
I eat my breakfast and start to get dressed
I adjust my collar to look my best
I head off to school
And see some people wearing sunglasses to try and look cool
The lessons that day were easy
Despite the fact I was feeling quite sneezy
When school was over I came home
And did my chores, which makes me moan
I turn on my Switch to play my game
Animal Crossing, that's the name
When it gets to bedtime I gaze at the sky
Wondering what it would be like to fly
When I think of the word 'night'
I think of the stars that shine 'o' so bright

But those stars aren't shining
They're really rocks burning
As I settle down to sleep, I think of what I could be
But for now, I just want to be me.

Molly Raybould (9)

I Am...

I am...
I am the one who holds all the strength, lingering in both my hands.
I am the relieved feeling of hope when your struggles are finally easy to understand.
I am the motivational speech inside the apostrophes that keep me safe and warm.
I am like the chamber of courage, but more like a dorm.
I am a lost soul when all glee is gone.
Like a piece of empty paper which resembles my heart that has been torn.
But nothing will ever stop me from gathering all my power.
I know that this 'disapproval' could never go on for hours.
With all these empowered people with their voices loud and strong.
I am and will be one of them and will bring everyone to the way they belong.
I am the person to never judge a book by its cover.
No one should ever doubt a person by race or colour.

So let your happy spirits and your opinions rise.
Because I am me, a girl who is only nine.

Varunikka Muraleekumar (10)

About Me

I like books and rainbows,
I like daffodils and stars,
I like friendship and happiness,
And I like chocolate bars.

My favourite food is doughnuts,
And I love books to read,
I'm really good at drawing,
And I'd love to plant a seed.

My hero is JK Rowling,
And I like Emma Watson too,
'Cause Harry Potter is the best,
And Ginny, I love you.

I find art very enjoyable,
And reading's good as well,
I love sketching pictures,
And I paint shells to sell.

I want to be an architect,
When I grow up,
I hope to help the environment,
And I really want a cute pup.

My favourite animal is a butterfly,
They're so pretty, don't you know?
I wish I could fly towards the sun,
The opposite of slow.

Elowen Doidge (9)

Sleep

As I went deeper into the dark and creepy bedroom, my senses started to fade,
I had enough that day and I wasn't going to lose it,
I had a cat, my parents, my siblings,
I had a dog, a hamster, and a mouse.
I couldn't let them all worry about me!

All of a sudden I felt a burst of adrenaline.
Off I went, not worrying one bit,
I walked with pride,
And entered my room that was to the side.
There was nothing to worry about as long as I was awake!

Then I realised that I was dreaming, nothing could be that good!
I felt something, smooth but fluffy at the same time.
It was calming me but I didn't feel calm.
It was my pillow!
I closed my eyes for a fleeting moment and opened them again,

I glanced outside and saw the sun shining over my room.
How had I fallen asleep that quick?!

Aisha Yusuf (10)

Nate

Hi, I'm Nate
I'm so great
The things that I hate
Are hard to calculate
So instead of telling
This story for a shilling
I do something I'm willing
That makes this poem top billing.
Literacy
It's part of me
Stories and poetry
Oh, the possibilities!
And next, there's PE, climbing a tree
Who dares to confront me?
I'm the #best
I'm the first in line
I'm even better than that there star you saw shine
And at the end of the day
When there's no school
I'd rather sit on a stool
Than stay up all day.

And in the morning, when I wake up
I really wish I had a little pup
To come up on my bed
And lick me on my head.
As I walk down to school
And wipe off the drool
Man, I look so cool
When it's the start of the day
You know I'm up to play!

Nathan Smith (9)

Just By Being Me

My hair shines brown, night-time and noon,
My eyes glint hazel, under the moon.

I sing, play guitar, write and read,
Planting, planting flowers, pulling up weeds.

I have many friends; I enjoy comedy and laughter,
I read Harry Potter, and happily ever after.

Art is my talent, I draw, sketch, observe,
Cluttering up my room is the paper I reserve.

I have a bed full of teddy bears I talk to when I'm sad,
A garden to play in, making games makes me glad.

I have a school I love, and a teacher I love more,
We do English and maths, activities galore.

I have an amazing family; perfect you could say,
I have three little brothers, kind and smart in every way.

So, I am Katie Hamilton, and here's what I want to be,
I feel special, loved and perfect, just by being me.

Katie Hamilton (10)

Me, As Can Be

Blue is my colour,
But it doesn't really suit me,
Cos I'm rarely in the doldrums,
If you ever see me.

Swimming and swimming,
Does it ever stop?
If you say yes then you're quite wrong,
Even though I love it,
I can't do it forever,
Eventually, I'll run out of fuel to carry on.

Do you know,
How I get chilli hot red?
If you know the answer,
You'll probably say
"It's your brother."

If you say that,
You're obviously wrong,
What gets on my nerves are tongue twisters!
Once they reach my tongue,
They go up to my brain and then I say it wrong.

Tennis is amazing,
However, I'm still not ten
But that wouldn't stop me, from hitting the ball
And run inside the court, without a fall.

All of the above is me, as me as can be!

Vaanika Sahajpal

This Is Me!

Hi, I'm Bradley and I am eight,
And I've got this brother I kinda hate.
But sometimes I've just got to live,
With the things that I was meant to be with.

I go to this amazing school,
Where there's learning crammed between every wall.
As soon as I just open the door,
The classroom's filled with science, geography, maths and more.

I've got some things I like to do,
Including playing 'It' with you.
I also like to play football,
In which I surely, totally rule.

I have five chickens who like to peck,
Juicy mealworm by the neck.
I also have a lovely dog,
Who likes to go on a little jog.

I like to draw and I'm really good,
Things that not all people could.
I also really love to write,
Which helped me finish this poem tonight!

Bradley Bowers (8)

Mother Earth (Global Warming)

Earth is crying non-stop day and night
I'm losing my breath, put the things right!

My trees are dying and my lands are sliding
It's painful reality, what's the point of hiding?

Food is short, birds and men are crying
My seas are dirty and my lakes are drying

I feel the heat, I can see flood and drought
My heart is aching, should I cry or shout?

Nests are birdless and honeycombs have no bees
Rainforest is on fire and you are cutting my trees

Digging coal, burning oil is making me shaky
I can't stand for long as I am weak and achy

Stop spreading carbon and act really fast
Think about the future and learn from the past.

Listen to Savannah's plea, use the globe sensibly
It's our Mother Earth, don't abuse her selfishly.

Savannah Javed (11)

My Mummy

Y ou make me smile and say, "Yippee!"
O r giggle joyfully with glee
U nderstand you're what makes me, me
R eally, we never disagree
E very day, we are happy

T o see you happy is so awesome
H ow can you be so pretty, like a blossom?
E verything would be pointless without you

B ecause you're so special, I can't live without you
E verything would be pointless without you
S o I'm writing this poem
T o make you cry

M ummy, I love you lots like Jelly Tots
U nderstand I'm what makes you, you
M ummy, I really, really love you.

Kaycie Bradbury (9)

Swan Sorrow

I am graceful like a swan,
Gliding across the water.
The stars twinkle,
And the moon shines.

The water softly ripples,
As a cherry blossom petal falls,
Indicating the start of spring.

The soft feather of sorrow,
Cuts through my heart.
Like a knife through butter.

Slowly disintegrating,
The feather floats through the pond of life,
Gone, but not forgotten.

As dawn breaks,
I rise.
My long feathers spread across.
My beautiful neck straightens.
My problems are gone.

The sun rises.
I lower my wings.
My feathers have a soft, warm glow.
It melts my sadness.
And I swim in my sorrow no longer.

Réiko McDonald (10)

Enthusiastic Me!

E nthusiastic like a monkey climbing the tallest tree
N ever gives up; always resilient
T he English language, RE and history are my favourite subjects to learn
H air, chestnut in colour and as long as a giraffe's neck
U tterly brilliant!
S pecial toys I like to keep safe and sound, tucked away in the garage
I spy with my little eye something beginning with A... Amazing!
A lways helping others
S wimming on a Thursday in the azure pool as fast as a shark with fluttering fins swimming for its prey
T otally awesome
I magination as gargantuan as an elephant's
C ool and calm and likes a good spa!

Aneel Kaur Kooner (9)

Happy Hope's Hilarious Poem

My name is Hope and I am nine,
I like art and I like to design.
My favourite colour is purple, my sister's is yellow,
I have a teacher at school, she's called Mrs Mellow.
Pandas are my favourite but so are fluffy dogs,
Although they're special creatures, I am scared of frogs!
My hair is as blonde as the golden sun,
Whenever I do a dancing show, I wear a bun.
At the weekend I play on the slip 'n' slide,
I start at the top and down the slide I glide!
When I'm older, I'll be a teacher or work at the vets,
I'm kind and caring and want to look after pets.
In my life, I have a million friends,
I always say friendship never ends.

Hope Boyle (9)

M.I.A, That's My Name

Who's that girl with the short brown hair?
Who's that girl looking up and down?
Who's that girl trying to look all small?
It's me, Mia
M.I.A, that's my name
M.I.A, that's my na a a me
Who's that girl with the pretty face?
Who's that girl with a book at break?
And who's that girl making friends so quick?
It's me, Mia
M.I.A, that's my name
M.I.A, that's my na a a me
Who's that girl that listens to everyone?
Who's that girl winning an election?
And who's that girl going home with Isa?
It's me, Mia
M.I.A, that's my name
M.I.A, that's my na a a me
Who is it?
Who is it?
Who is it?

What's your name?
Mia
M.I.A, that's my name
Yo!

Mia Godfrey (9)

My Unstoppable Mind

I sit upon my windowsill,
The trees are rustling, nothing's still.

Not even my brain.

Fairy tales are flooding in,
My mind is ideas rattling in a tin.
Dragons and lands from way up high,
My thoughts are drifting to the sky.

I mutter in the supermarket,
I think of a story and how to start it.
My ideas are bubbles being consumed in my mind,
They tickle and wriggle and pop at random times.

I watch dreamily at the clock in the middle of a test,
Then I tell my brain "Will you give it a rest!?"
My mind whirs like a washing machine,
Taking adjectives and making them clean.

Cogs turning, constantly working.

I love to think of what to write,
Though a full story of mine has never been in sight.

Scarlett Milbourne (10)

This Is Me

I am a superstar swimmer in the pool and in the sea,
I am a sea life lover,
I love land creatures too,
I love singing and dancing, piano and art,
These are the things that fill up my heart.

I've got chocolate-brown eyes and dark blonde hair,
That glimmers in the sun and blows in the air,
My feeling is happy, cheery and fun,
I love to bounce on my trampoline or head out for a bun.

I was born in December 2012,
A winter baby, that's me,
I love to snuggle up in front of the fire,
Watch a movie and eat s'mores with my family,
Summer's good too,
Staying up late enjoying a bright warm evening,
Going on holidays,
Eating ice lollies,

All of it...
It's the best.

Hannah McMurray (9)

Liam's Wonderful World

My name's Liam and I'm eleven,
I'm in year six, nearly year seven.
I've got two dogs: Rossi and Ellie,
Every day I tickle their belly!
At Sports Day this year we won the cup,
Because I'm the house captain I lifted it up!
In my spare time I play the Xbox,
In lots of the games they race over rocks.
With my family, I'm going on holiday,
In the pool I like to play.
My favourite food is pizza and swordfish!
Not together because that'd be a weird dish!
My birthday this year was at Chill Factory!
Everyone sang happy birthday to me!
I'm Liam and I'm kind, lost things I always find.

Liam O'Connor (11)

We Are All Unique

We are all unique
A growing tree, a blooming flower, from seed to bud to blossom,
We all look the same on the outside but we are all different inside,
We are all baby birds taking flight,
Listening and learning to the call of the night,
As our knowledge expands, we do too,
Our brain gathers all information and stores it away like a radio station.

The aquamarine fish snatcher swooping down from his perch becomes a blurring web of colour.
Speckled aqua, cyan, white and rusty chestnut brown,
The daring king has to stay out of reach of the fighting northern river pike to catch his little sticklebacks.
This is survival; the beauty of life -
We all have to persevere.

Zelphi Fine Naidu (11)

Things I Like!

I like my birthday because we all celebrate,
And share the memories that we all create,
And it's always a good happily ever after.
I also like my family because we can share our feelings,
And they can be very appealing.
I also like eating because it makes you happy,
And you can always clean your mouth with your hanky.
I very much like going to school because I like education,
And when you come back you are filled with anticipation,
I also like my teachers, they give the time to teach us,
And let us be us.
I like flowers, that beautifully bloom under the magnificent sun
Red, blue, green but my favourite is the bright purple tulips.

This is why I love my life!

Navleen Kaur

Give And Take

I give you glittering, glorious gold
You give me old, scraped copper
I give you shining, shimmering sapphires
You give me worse, dirty water

I give you fantastic full-coloured flowers
You give me revolting, dirty soil
I give you marvellous mountains
You give me horrifying, heavy avalanches

I give you colourful, bright swarms of fishes
You give me wild, dangerous tsunamis
I give you huge blue whales
You give me bone-shattering megalodons

I give you life-durable love
You give me saddening, horrid grief
I give you the wonders of life
You give me the silent, deathly death.

Isabella Nikolov (8)

What Could I Be?

I was sitting there thinking one day
And I said, "What could I be?" So then I also said,
I could be a diver that swims all through the sea,
Studies coral all day and reports back to the bay,
Or a pilot that flies all through the sky,
Watches birds fly high and drives planes through the night,
And maybe a swimmer that wins lots of races,
Goes to the Olympics and steals all the places,
Or maybe an athlete that's faster than Bolt,
That's also the fastest there so you might as well go home.
But then I thought of the perfect job, being me.
I know it sounds weird to you but the quickest, easiest and best to be...
Is me!

Erika Middleton (9)

Rubik's Cube Fun!

R acing my dad and my friends is so much fun
U nder time pressure, I must get it done
B est of all is that I get to play and learn
I f I practise every day, I feel less concern
K nowing the algorithm helps me solve the puzzle in a very fast time
S peed cubes are my favourite type, just like my home-made slime

C arefully and skillfully, I twist and turn the colourful cube
U sually, I enjoy playing on the London tube
B attling to win time challenges with my friends
E xcited and happy when I solve the Rubik's cube in the end.

Jasmin Sehdev (9)

This Is Me

This is me
Who am I?
Well, I am a young girl,
Who aspires to be a doctor one day.

Why?
I love looking after people,
That's why!

From a young age,
Playing doctors and nurses was my favourite game,
Oh, I loved it when they changed my name.

In my spare time,
I love to write,
About monsters who like to bite.

Beowulf,
Frankenstein,
Dracula,
Are my favourite friends,
I love it how their fate ends.

My friends call me sporty,
As well as crazy,
But my parents call me lazy,
How rude!

In summary, I am awesome,
I don't want to change who I am,
If you make me change the way I am,
Let's just say I will turn into the next Beowulf...

Bhargavi Rajanikanth (10)

My Sadness, Tucked Away

M y sadness gets forgotten in cherishing moments
I ncredibly hated my sadness is
S ometimes though, he just creeps out when something upsets me
E ven when everyone else is joyful but me, he manages to make them unhappy too
R eally, he burst out in 2020
A nd now I have nothing to be down-hearted about, so he's tucked away, deep inside me
B ut sometimes he escapes and collaborates with anger and frustration
L azy is what he is now, and I hope he stays like that for a long time
E ither that or he's extremely undercover!

Nyma Jawwad (11)

This Is Me

I go home and rest all day,
All I do is play my game.
I enjoy school and learning too
But it's boring and it's tiring too.
My friends and I always play
No matter what the weather's like that day.
I like to play football but I'm bad
And sometimes that makes me feel sad.
I have lots of friends to play with so it's hard to play with one, you see
I have lots who aren't friends like me.
Wet socks are annoying and I try
And let them dry
Before I go out
And about.
This poem is all about me
And this is the end, can't you see?

Georgia-Mae Smith (10)

This Is Me

I am Sophia,
Sophia I am,
I live in a place,
Across the land.

I am a sister,
The best that can be,
To my dear brother, Raffi,
Who is annoying to me!

I am a daughter,
My parents are great,
They cook me my dinner,
But sometimes it's late.

I am a school child,
The teacher's pet to be exact,
My teacher, Miss Sen,
Loves me in fact.

I am a friend,
Caring and kind,
I'll always be there for them,
Our friendships entwined.

I am a dancer,
The craziest around,
My friends watch me perform,
As I prance along the ground.

I am Sophia,
Happy and brave,
I love my life greatly,
I'll end with a wave.

Sophia Piper (10)

A Recipe To Bake Me!

To bake me, you will need:
A teaspoon of kindness
A jar of love
A cupboard full of books
5ml of helpfulness
A cup full of honesty
A bottle of respect
A bowl of teamwork
A flask filled with lemon water.

Now you need to:
Pour the cup full of honesty into a pot
Then pour in the bowl of teamwork
Add the jar of love
Let me be cooked for some minutes!
Pour in the bottle of respect
Cook me for 5 minutes
Put in 5ml of helpfulness
Add the teaspoon of kindness
Finish cooking me!
Add the cupboard full of books.
Finally, pour some of the lemon water into the pot.

Watch me emerge from the pot!
This is me!

Janna Oyedeji (9)

Doubtful Dreams

Floating in ice cream
Is it my dream?

It might have been long ago,
But now everything is not Lego.

Now I am mature,
Knowing the nature.

Working to be a genius
Or am I dreaming to be ingenious?

Should I be a mathematician?
Or should I be a magician?

Is it a question?
Or is it a mission?

Should I join a team?
Or should I just dream?

Should I swim like a trout in freshwater?
All my dreams are in doubt.

But I will never give up.
I will be like a tiger cub.

I am a team member,
A person who everyone will remember.

Never following any footsteps,
I will always go up by steps.

This is me!

Aradhya Adeesh (9)

The Route I Take

Two roads emerged,
One had broken bottles
Smashed against the ground,
The other path was covered in tall,
Emerald grass,
That was what urged me
To walk that path.

The luscious green grass
Attracted me,
It induced me to think
I would find something unique,
I took that route;
I was not disappointed.

The glass attracted them
But did not appeal to me,
Curiosity got the better of them
And let their guard down.
They took that route;
And they were satisfied.

Just because they walked that path,
Doesn't mean you must follow,
Have some dignity;
Follow your heart

It's okay to be different.

Faith Umeadi (11)

Hopes And Dreams

I wanted to be a doctor
That was bad luck
I snuck into the blood room
And boom, I fainted

I wanted to be a dancer
I fell off the stage
I'm such a clutz
With very bad luck

I wanted to be a singer
But I can't sing
I sound like a frog
And my high notes aren't very long

I wanted to be a scientist
I failed the class
That was a blast
But I ended up in a cast

The truth is I'm not very good at anything
No singing, dancing
Even contemporary

My talent is hidden, waiting to be discovered
Like a snail in its shell
This is me with zero talents
But who am I to judge.

Oyinlola Fadairo (9)

Who I Want To Be

I wonder, I ponder,
Is this the real me?
A young girl,
As sweet as can be.
Or is it just a lie,
Beneath my skin,
Waiting to be told again?

I grab my pencil,
And write away,
Hoping to become an author one day.
I cannot conclude,
If that's what I should do,
So little steps are all I breathe,
Therefore, until my mind agrees.

I wonder, I ponder,
Is this the real me?
An intelligent, pragmatic girl,
As kind as can be.
A little inspiration is all I need,
To overcome the shy cage surrounding me,

But one thing is sure,
Becoming an author is all I want to achieve!

Hoda Ahmed (11)

This Is Me

My eyes are wobbly
And softly roll around
When I am tired
Or have done hard work.

Everything is fuzzy.
When people point things out to me
I get disappointed
Because I can't see things far away.

I like to wear bows in my fringe
Skirts, shorts and tights
My hair is always up
In plaited pigtails or a ponytail.

I love to do Pokémon cards with my sister
And play Sylvanian families
Me and my friends laugh about pie
Usually my gramps and I do models together, making houses, a cinema and even a road from cardboard.

This is me.
I wouldn't change anything.

Olivia Marsh (7)

My Dream Is To Become A Footballer

My dream is to become a footballer
A footballer I shall be
I'll tackle and shoot
With my golden boot
For a footballer I shall be

My dream is to become a footballer
A footballer I shall be
I'll score all the goals and hattricks
I'll do some fancy flicks
For a footballer I shall be

My dream is to become a footballer
A footballer I shall be
I'll set up goals galore
I'll tackle them to the floor
For a footballer I shall be

My dream is to become a footballer
A footballer I shall be
So the world can see
The footballer I can grow up to be.

Isabelle Jordan (9)

My Favourite Things

Fish are golden. Fish are bright,
I love my fish, my company at night.

Ice cream is fantastic. Ice cream's so cold,
Mint chocolate chip's my favourite, even at nine years old.

Drawing is fun. Drawing's the best,
It's okay to mess up, some say I'm obsessed.

Dancing is amazing. Dancing is my dream,
I like to be together, with friends in my team.

My brother's name is Jenson. He likes to make me laugh,
We play every day and smile for our photographs.

The excitement that all of these bring,
I feel so lucky to have my favourite things.

Amelia Curley (9)

The Writer's Dream!

I love roller coasters,
I like ice cream,
I hate Twitter,
Dark chocolate is too bitter,
I like to pretend to be an explorer,
Scouring through the jungle I go,
I climb all the mountains and trees,
I always get up when I fall on my knees,
I love reading those action books,
I also love writing stories more than anyone else,
I have a dream to be a writer,
A writer who writes stories of old,
A writer who writes stories of bold,
A writer who helps people's dreams come true,
I like being fun and adventurous too,
So let's give me a great "Woo hoo!"

Millie Guyll-Wiggins (11)

Great Grace!

My name is Grace and I'm seven (nearly eight).
I like doing English - I am great!
My favourite colour is shiny sunset yellow.
I like it when the sun says hello!
My gramps makes the best green, healthy soup.
It's spicy and yummy and not like gloop!
I play with my sister; we make slime.
When I go to the park, I like to climb.
When I'm older, I want to teach in a beautiful, calm school.
I think this will be super cool!
My name's Grace and I'm nearly eight.
I might be tiny but I am great!

Grace Boyle (7)

Me

My name is Phoebe,
But I'll go by Pheebs,
As long as you're my friend, that is,
And here are some facts about me!

I'd love to be an author,
And write my creative mind,
Three words that describe me are,
Beautiful, quiet and kind.

I'd love to travel the world,
And I love being by the sea,
The raging waves and soft sand,
Is where I would like to be.

I love writing poetry,
It helps me think more carefully,
I hope you liked this poem,
All about me!

Phoebe Stanford (10)

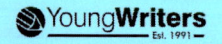

Try

That was the day that one of the most important people in my life died,
It was from a disease,
I was told that it would be okay,
That everything was going to be fine,
When I was told, I stood there motionless,
As if underwater,
I would not believe it,
I could not believe it,
I tried to imagine it wasn't true,
It was a dream,
But deep down I knew that it was,
I have carried on my life,
Missing her, but trying to be happy,
Because if you're not happy,
You won't have a happy life,
And I know that she would want me to be happy,
Always.

Lila Barasi (10)

This Is Me

I have brown hair and eyes
And that's a fact, no lies.
My favourite colour's black,
Violin is my knack.
I am one of a kind,
So keep that in mind.
I am described as smart
And I really love art.
I have a family of big hearts,
That can never fall apart.
So that's who I am,
Sweet as a lamb.
I always pass my exams,
And love peanut butter and jam.
I never show any disrespect,
I would love to become an architect.
Yet there is no one I'd rather be
Than me.

Lianne Bnouni (11)

My Moment

My contentful moment
Is when I say delightful comments.
My happy minute
Is when I receive merits.

My amusing moment
Is when I do an enormous movement.
My funny minutes
Could be when someone flies a lot of rockets.

My miserable moment
Is when I get nasty punishment.
My sad minute
Is when people bully me at the market.

My frightened moment
Is when I do an advertisement.
My terrified minute
Is when I go over the limits.

My enjoyable moment
Is when I play instruments.
My pleasing minute
Is when I look after my pets.

This is me
As you can see.

Azhahinii Ravishankar (9)

This Is Me

Balls and friends
The things I love the most
I like In For A Penny
With the funny TV host

I like to be bright and vibrant
Tie-dye is the best
Although it makes a lot of mess
My art has really progressed

I like to dance and sing
With my big sis
When she is gone I miss her
Mostly because she gives me a big kiss

My cat bites
My cat licks
She dances to the videos
Done by Joe Wicks

I like gymnastics
It's so great
I can do a cartwheel
Like my best mate

Chocolate and crisps
Burgers and fries
I like food
When it's a surprise

This is me!

Esme Yates

This Is Me

This is me
I've got black hair
I've got black eyes
And I've got flair.

I like dresses
I like the rain
I don't like sleep
I don't like pain.

I run around
And play all day
On weekends
There's more time to play!

I enter lots of
Competitions
Mainly 'cause I've got
Serious ambitions!

I've got a brother
He's called Sami
He never stops
Annoying me!

My mum and dad
Are very clever
They're never wrong
Just never ever!

So now you've learnt
A lot about me
Let's chat about you
And have some tea!

Mimi Tian (8)

My Emotions

My emotions sometimes bottle up
I cry, not just with happiness but tears of sadness, nervousness and fear
Once when I felt judged, I trudged along fields
When I feel joy, I play with my pet and say, "Good boy!"
When people make me feel sad, I start to feel a little mad
My emotions, my emotions, these are my emotions
When I feel sick, I'm never strong enough to kick a ball
So if you feel sad, don't feel like you're bad
If that doesn't help, and you give a little welp
Just remember, it's something everyone feels.

Ava Swift (10)

Someday I Will Be An Artist

I won't ever be an artist
Like Pablo Picasso or Monet
When my pen touches the paper
I scribble it up and throw it away

All my friends say I'm a good artist
But I don't really think it's true
Maybe I should just give it up
And start another hobby anew

But I love drawing, it's my passion
Artists for the win!
Maybe I could just believe in myself
And not throw it in the bin

One day I *will* be an artist
Just like Pablo Picasso and Monet
Just like other artists before me
My art has something to say.

Kaiyah-Rayne Garratt (10)

This Is Me

T his is me;
H appy and smiley
I maginative and crafty
S mart and resilient

I ndustrious and independent
S ister of two

M indful and caring
E nthusiastic and entertaining

A dventurous and brave
A doring and loving
I nventive and confident
E mpathetic and passionate
S upportive and sincere
H onourable and helpful
A dmirable and advancing.

Aaiesha Mohamed Faizal (10)

We're All Imperfect!

Some people are imperfect,
Just like me, but in their own ways,
While some people are perfect,
Don't believe? Then check out their stuff and trays.

I am one of the imperfect!
And I'm stuck on my own line,
Don't worry, you're not the only one imperfect
We're all stuck in our own time!

No one is always perfect!
Don't worry, you're not the only one,
We are all imperfect!
And always the messy one!

We're not always perfect,
We're also imperfect!

And so this is *me!*

Anna Wieckiewicz (10)

This Is Me

I am creative,
I like sports,
I like drawing,
Falcons and hawks.

I like being out in the sun,
I like playing on my Xbox One,
I like being with my friends all day,
I like going on my iPad to play.

I like going out to the shop,
I like eating lollipops,
I am tired after school,
I wish I had a big pool.

I like the things that are about me,
I like things that are super clean,
I like people that are smart,
I like being at home throwing darts.

This is a poem,
That I have made,
This is my final verse,
For today.

Christopher Regha (8)

My Amazing Personality

A rtist - This is who I am when I use my creation
K ind - I am nice to my friends in any situation
S upportive - Failures happen but they don't let me down
H onest - Being truthful can avoid having a frown
I maginative - House talking, sofa walking, don't seem true
T houghtful - Reading books and sharing ideas help my crew
H opeful - Believing in self will always lead to success
A dventurous - Being brave and fearless can definitely impress.

Akshitha Arun Prasanth (8)

My Riddle

Who is the Monopoly menace in your house?
Who is the Netflix streamer in your house?
Who is the keyboard rattler in your house?
Who is the book basher in your house?
Who is the paintball patroller in your house?
Who is the sushi slicer in your house?
Who is the continent conqueror in your house?
Who is the drum basher in your house?
Who is the music appreciator in your house?
Who is the amazing adventurer in your house?
Because in my house... that is me!

Isaac De Vilder (11)

Being Finnlay

I'm a brilliant big brother,
Kind and caring like a teddy bear,
Curly hair like a fluffy sheep,
And a top team player.

I am a fantastic footballer and I'm known as Little Giggs,
Cricket, rugby, biking, running, I love sport!
I like to design Lego.
I am a drawing genius.

I love eating gammon, Haribo, ice cream, biscuits,
They are delicious and scrumdiddlyumptious,
But my favourite is Fanta,
It's amazing, fizzy and delicious.

Finnlay Annetts (9)

Where Am I?

Spending time with my fun cousins
And eating lots of food and swimming in the day.
Going to yummy, delicious restaurants, eating lots and lots of fish,
Especially eating my favourite, awesome clams.
Where do you think I am?

I will tell you it's very hot,
It's a special holiday for me because it's where I am from.
I love going to Alemeda Park
Where I can play and see tropical trees
And spin around and around on a merry-go-round.

Aaron Skandarajah-Vazquez (8)

ABC Me

A is for apples,
B is for bats,
C is for chickens,
D is for Doja Cat.

E is for elephants,
F is for friends,
G is for grapes,
H is for hens.

I is for Irish,
J is for jams,
K is for kangaroos,
L is for lambs.

M is for Miss Humphries,
N is for nice,
O is for oats,
P is for precise.

Q is for quizzes,
R is for rain,
S is for skating,
T is for trains.

U is for ukuleles,
V is for vibraphones,
W is for water,
X is for xylophones.

Y is for yaks,
Z is for zoo,
When I write poems,
I never feel blue.

Skyla Washington (11)

Life Isen't Easy

Life isen't as easy as it sounds,
Dyslexier macks it worse.
Bullying and teasing bring me down
Teachers who don't know are a curse.

When someone ses it's easy to read
I silenty cry on my own.
Werds dance about even thouh I pleed,
I silenty cry all alone.

But the thing I truely hate is when
Some idiot ses: What's the matter?
Can't you remember? Pick up your pen and spell
idiot.

Connie Allen (11)

Somewhere Different

I used to live in Africa
It felt like home
Now I have moved, I feel safe but more alone
Now we are here, everything seems crazy
I hope my memories don't become hazy
I'll keep my memories forever
I hope they don't fade, not ever.
Sometimes it's sad, sometimes I'm glad
And sometimes even a bit mad

After a bit of thinking, I want to tell you
Home's everywhere but my heart's still there
Don't worry because I'll still visit
Thank you, that's it!

Anaya Smart (9)

Foreshadowing Demise

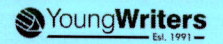

Foreshadowing demise...
Under the deck, the cabin lies
Can't you hear the gulls cry?
Lucky for us, the night fades away
The gulls seek their prey...
Night is gone
Soon comes day
Killer gulls kept at bay.

Dawn is on time
As I throw my last dime
The darkness above
It shows enough
Death obeys its order
The ship is in the depths.

The smell of rotten food
Obstructs the salty air
Like a plague
Spreading like wildfire
Rats scurry for shelter
As the waters swish

Back
And
Forward.

William Bolton (10)

I Have ADHD

This is me
I have ADHD!

I sometimes shout,
But I like you to know all the things I know about.

I sometimes struggle to sit still,
But I can have times when I chill.

I have a pet cat,
She sits on my lap and likes a pat.

I'm loved by my family so much,
I was made with love, and God's touch.

I am often loud,
But all the things I am, and do make me proud.

This is me!

Thomas Moore (10)

My Life

I am Charlie,
I have four siblings,
My parents are married,
My family is great!
There are twenty-six people in my class,
Everyone is my friend,
The teachers are outstanding,
Said Ofsted!
I used to hide my feelings,
Neither happy nor sad,
They all mixed together,
Until I couldn't take it anymore.
Then my family came,
And friends, and teachers,
And all came together,
Only to make me better!

Charlie Dimelow (9)

This Is Me

M y name is Maria Miah, star of the sea
A rrietty is my most-watched film
R eading is like a roller coaster full of fun and facts
I bake, I am a baker, I bake pizza
A lways full of imaginative ideas

M angoes are sweet, as sweet as my friends
I deally trips to the beach are the best for me
A lways ensuring endless love for my family
H elpful is the name for me.

Maria Miah (10)

Carefree

I'm quite the girl you see,
Unbothered and carefree.
Just like you, I'm me
Different from everybody else yes, please
My name is Regina, means I'm a queen
I've got coils and twists, woven and well-chosen
My eyes are brown like rubies and sapphires buried deep beneath the ground
One old, one young, two sisters in the house
Should see their moves, could bust your eyes out
Chatter, chatter, chatter, could talk all day
Can you stop?
No way!

Regina Jalloh

My Life As A Stammerer

I stutter
I stammer
So please be polite
Don't finish my sentences
Every night.

Sometimes I put too much
Strain on my words
I force them out
But they don't want to be heard.
However, you would be surprised
At the impact the stammer has on my life.

I don't know
Why I care
Don't know why
I don't dare
To speak aloud
Just be my friend
Take me as I am
All the teasing needs to end.

This is my life
With my stammer
And my strife!

Thomas Whitting

A Previous Life

Sometimes I sit and wonder if
I had a life before my own.
Sometimes I sit and wonder if
I had a life I've never known.
I could've had a life where
I was a block of cheese.
I could've had a life where
I was a plate of peas.
I could've had a life where
I was good at pottery.
I could've had a life where
I had won the lottery.
I could've had a life where
I was a butter knife.
But if I'm being honest
I like my current life.

Milo Pollard (9)

One Of A Kind

I'm brave
I'm strong
I'm fearless.
I'm curious,
Weird
And funny.
I'm trustworthy
I'm eager
And I'm... I'm me.

When I shine like a star, I say to myself, "That's who you really are."
And all those things, even the bad things, make me one of a kind.
What's more, that one of a kind helps me find myself in my mind.
And there's only one person allowed in my world
That's me
So, myself only...

Zofia Lewandowska (10)

Someone I Admire

C ourageous, kept going with every single step
A dmired by lots of people
P erseverance means never giving up
T eamwork, working together
A ll across the world his story was heard
I nspiring other people
N oticing that something needed to change

T aking pride in what he did
O ver 32 million pounds he raised
M ore people were inspired.

Lucy Pankhurst (8)

Magnificent Me

I am like a tall tree,
With magnificent leaves.
Oh, magnificent me.

I am like the swervy sea,
With gigantic waves.
Oh, magnificent me.

I am like the whooshing wind,
That blows from the west.
Oh, magnificent me.

I am like the rapid drops of rain,
That falls on the land.
Oh, magnificent me.

I am like the flash of lightning
That bolts across the angry sky.
Oh, magnificent me.

All of God's creations are part of magnificent me!

Elliot Newman (8)

All About Me

I've got a sharp mind,
And I'm very, very kind.
My hair is very long,
And I'm very fit and strong.
I am very sporty,
And a little bit naughty.
I'm very funny,
But I really want a bunny.
I have a big smile,
And I can kick a ball a mile.
I put my personality on this page,
And my writing is an open cage.
I shine like a star,
And I hope my poem goes far.

Jemima Clifford (9)

Who Am I?

K ind as can be, helping everyone I can
A ctively curious about challenges to come
A rtistically creating things from imagination
V arious colours I fly with
I n the day or night
N urturing everyone
I can, with proudness inside me from
Y ellow sun to the white moon
A ll around the world
L ovely and caring I shall be forever!

Kaaviniyal Ilanthendral (9)

This Is Me

A mazing Anaya - that is my name
N ever in my life have I owned a pet
A nnoyingly messy is my middle name
Y awning in boredom through endless homework
A wesome at baking - my speciality

K han is the name for kings
H abitually annoying my brother everywhere
A thletically aggressive at netball
N ervous to go to secondary school.

Anaya Khan (9)

Dancer

D ancing is my hobby, it's what I like to do
A nd in dance class, I have loads of friends who dance with me too
N ever give up, never quit, even if I can't get it right
C linton is my dance teacher, with practice it will soon be right!
E vie and Imogen are my friends, we dance together and the fun never ends
R ehearsals get us ready for the big finale show!

Seren Grace Joy-Rooney (9)

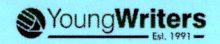

My Imagination

Imagination is my thing,
My ideas always go *ping!*
I imagine myself in a lonely wood,
Nothing in here seems very good,
I imagine myself hungry in the middle of the sea,
Eating just one single pea,
I imagine there's a person in a beautiful forest,
Picking flowers for a florist,
I imagine myself on a hot, sunny beach,
With an ice cream always just out of reach,
I wake up from my dream,
Exactly at 7:13.

John Griffiths (8)

This Is Me!

I'm not loud, I'm not quiet, I'm somewhere in the middle,
I chat, chat, chat to my friends, they say I talk in riddles.
I love to read, write and draw,
Do gymnastics, dance, and so much more.
I'd say I'm kind and polite,
And the teachers say I'm bright.
To become an author is my dream,
And to succeed would make me beam.
I always try to be the best I can be,
And that is just to be me!

Josie Day (11)

How To Make Alfie

Add a smile as bright as the sun.
Next, sprinkle in some imagination.
On top of that pour in some kindness and care.
Add three whole spoonfuls of hard work to get the job done.
Then add some dashes of rugby, swimming and football.
A packet of friendliness and sharing.
Last of all, a drop of red.
Mix it all together, then roll it out and you will have your very own Alfie.

Alfie Summerfield (8)

This Is Me

T rains are my favourite transport,
H appy, I always try to stay contended,
I personally like ghee dosa as my favourite food,
S alah is my favourite football player,

I love baking and building Lego,
S age-green is my favourite colour,

M y friends are very supportive,
E very day I play piano and guitar.

Anjayen Ananda (10)

What Is The ZoZo Way?

What is the ZoZo way?
It takes a bit of energy, with a bit of skill,
Now don't forget the flexibility, or you'll stay still.
You can see me hanging on the monkey bars,
Or climbing like a chimpanzee.

But that is not all ZoZo can do, she can split like the sea,
Move aside as she cartwheels like a little pea.
That is the ZoZo way, come join us for tea.
We'll have fun you see,
Shall we?

Zoya Iqbal (9)

Nature And Me

The nature love that makes up me,
Is of the hovering honeybee.
It's of the moon, that milk-white char.
It's of the midnight, that never-ending smear of tar.

It's of the sun, that star ablaze,
That lights our world in many ways!
The flowers that bloom and smell so sweet,
They burst into life in the summer heat.

The glint of sparkling diamond sea,
That makes up such a part of me.

Isla Aitken (9)

Magnificent Me

M agnificent me
A mazing, talented swimmer
G reat at art
N osy
I n all things as elegant as a ballerina
F unny to the bone
I ntimidated by no one
C ooking and baking spontaneously
E xtraordinarily thick long hair
N umber-one granddaughter
T rouble is my middle name.

Arsh Khan (10)

Being Me

Being me is good.
I like to be kind.
When I am told, I don't make a sound.
I am like a happy cloud because I cheer others up.

I wear glasses,
In my guitar classes.
I know how to do my laces.
I'm going to get braces.

I'm born in Britain.
I love my kitten.
I hate bears,
Because they are scary.

Yousef Aburadi

This Is Me

D aniel is my name,
A ction-adventure, I love to game,
N oodles I like,
I love to ride my bike,
E very day at school,
L ovely food makes me drool.

M oney for every chore,
O ften is a bore,
O utstanding at bike riding,
R ide as fast as lightning,
E very day be kind, the world is nice you'll find.

Daniel Moore (11)

Who Am I?

I am I
Son of Mum
Who loves kindness
Who hates unfairness
Who admires Mum for her unconditional love
Who fears the big bad wolf
Who dreams of being a cute sheep
Who needs braveness to face challenges
Maths magician of 3AO
Good teammate of my football team
Best friend of Artie
Sweet boy of Mum
I am Sky.

Sky Kwok (8)

You're A Star

Some people say,
"You're not good enough"
But the good people say
"You are amazing."

If you believe in yourself
Then you can do anything.
I like my funny features
And my smart self
In fact, I like everything.

Try your best
In what you do
Maybe you can end up
Like me
And have courage and pride,
Just wait and see!

Eva Wright (8)

Artistic

A rt is an amazing thing
R ight to left my paintbrush strokes
T aking my time, a creation forms
I 'm in a new and beautiful galaxy
S hining in my own way
T hrough my painting, I come alive
I 'm walking in a dream
C olours burst out as I brush the last time.

Seren Smart (11)

Excitement

Excitement is like a roller coaster,
You go to the top and your heart pounds,
When you fall to the bottom your insides scream,
The roller coaster is a tangerine orange,
In a forest full of trees,
Where the plants and animals thrive,
Nothing more beautiful in the whole, entire world,
This is a roller coaster that brings joy where it travels.

Oliver Cross-Monaghan (10)

The Darkest Hour

Didn't have a good start to life
From every direction came a knife
Jabbing at my heart
Just want to restart
I need salvation
I need affirmation
Living on the edge
I'm becoming wedged
Falling down a hole
Can't get out again
Now alone in the dark
Just need a bright spark
Then I curl up in a ball
Because no one comes
When I call.

Josh Townsend

Proud To Be Me

'Unique' is the meaning of my name
Football definitely is my favourite game
Passionate with dreams as lofty as sky
Always exuberant and keen to try
I'm not a worrysaurus, I stay cool
I'm not a nerd but I still love school
I don't follow others, and feel proud to be me
Always striving to be a better version of me.

Fareed Ahmed (8)

Qualities Of Ayden Panesar

A lways ready to help
Y outhful and unique
D oesn't be rude
E nthusiastic
N ot selfish

P layful
A lways understanding
N ever gives up
E nergetic
S olving problems
A lways happy
R eady to learn.

Ayden Panesar (10)

This Is Me

Z ahra is my name
A pples are my favourite
H opping is my thing
R ainbows are cool
A lex is my friend

M iah is my last name
I love my family
A rrietty is my most loved character
H owl's Moving Castle is my second loved film.

Zahra Miah (8)

Who Am I?

I have a poorly heart
But that's not me
I struggle to remember
But that's not me
I go to hospital a lot
But that's not me
I love Aston Villa
That's me
I love art
That's me
I love playing with my friends
That's me
Who am I?
I am Alfie.

Alfie Donnelly (9)

We Had Covid

Cough, cough went my mom.
We had Covid
And we were all stuck at home.
I would have been
Excited had it been during school,
But it was half term.
Asher and Teddy (who are my siblings) were meant
to go to Winter Wonderland.
Instead, I called my friends (Olivia C and Joely)
And played Roblox.

Olivia Lauffer

Bugatti Veyron

My Bugatti Veyron can go fast
Cheetah is what it can go past

My Bugatti Veyron is cool
But it can't go in the pool

My Bugatti Veyron is well made
I am glad that it's fully paid

My Bugatti Veyron is advanced
Don't worry, you could have a glance.

Omar Faisal (7)

Ellis Is My Name

E llis is my name and my favourite colour is orange
L ittle I am, my mum calls me her little dot
L ots of food I like; bananas, oranges, ribs and rice are some of them
I love my friends and family
S wimming is one of my favourite sports, I also like kickboxing.

Ellis Edwards (7)

The Recipe Of Me

A sprinkle of madness,
A touch of sadness,
A spoonful of work,
A scoop of beserk,
A gram of care,
A kilogram of share,
A cup of dare,
A bowl of writing,
A litre of fighting,
A plate of love,
She can climb above,
Some time to read,
And that makes me!

Avni Saraswathi (8)

Brightness And Darkness

What is darkness?
Darkness is what haunts you at night
Darkness is the invisibility cloak for robbers at night
There is only one thing that can conquer it, and that is brightness
Brightness is an alarm that exposes the robbers
Brightness is the fire that lights up the whole world.

Michael Neeman (10)

This Is Me

T urbo as a jet in sports
H appy playing PES 2022
I nterested in literacy
S ports, all ears

I nsecure about art
S cience is my speciality

M aths is my strong hand
E ven when I am older I will never change.

Kavithan Davidprapakaran (8)

This Is Me

I'm the beating heart inside.
I'm the smile that's on everyone's face.
I'm your favourite show that cheers you up, that will solve the case.
I am the laugh when you spend time with your family.
I'm the food that satisfies your stomach yummily.
I am me.

Kai Hendricks Bryant

How Do I Feel?

When I am jumping on the trampoline,
In my top and jean.
When I am playing football,
And giving it my all.
When I am at the beach,
And for the shells I reach.
When I am playing games,
And finish all my aims.
When I see a slithery snake,
A real one, not a fake.
How do I feel?

Answer: Happy!

Binyamin Bhamji (9)

A Mirror Of Me!

Look in a mirror,
What do you see?
I see everything that defines me,
Every part is celebrated,
Inside and out!
No need to be as pure as a summer's day,
To celebrate me and to have a great day,
I love me in every way,
My imagination runs wild and free,
This is what is so amazing about me!

Liza Hussain

The Days Of The Show

You act your part, as amazing as you are,
Free yourself, don't hold back anymore,
You have the talent, more than any actress,
You cherish every moment,
The day to leave is a complete misery,
But keep going,
Next year, you have a chance,
Now you know me!

Himavarsha Manchikanti (9)

Marvellous Me

There is only one me in the world,
The special way my hair is curled.
My eyes are like ebony coal
And I have a very distinctive mole.
I am tall for my age
And my skin is warmish beige.
My wit is quick
And my hair is thick.
I am an adventurous guy
And I love to fly.
This is marvellous me.

Dylan Gill (11)

At Nine

I am now nine.
I enjoy being kind.
I'm exploring all the time.
Making new skills by learning to find my way through a world that can be hard to walk the line.
I fight with the ways and mistakes grow in my mind.
To be all I can helps me become divine and makes me feel sublime.

Jasper Cashman (9)

A Poem About Me

S ad is my least favourite feeling,
U nderneath the covers of my bed is my favourite place,
S ushi is my favourite food,
H appy is what I feel when I'm reading a book or playing with my dog,
I love surfing the snow on skis.

Henry Miller (9)

Halloween Here

H appy monsters
A ll around us
L aughing happily
L oving the darkness
O utside is where the fun begins
W aiting for the scary masks
E ating sweets
E veryone is happy
N o more Halloween.

Kai Runaghan

Reading

R eady to read
E very day I read a few pages
A lways learning new words
D ifferent words can make writing much better
I love reading
N o days without any reading
G o to the library to read different books.

Ruiwen Gong (8)

Nathan Rap

Nathan is my name,
I really love to game.
For Fortnite levels I grind,
Geocaches I find.
I really, really like,
To ride fast on my bike.
Or on my electric scooter,
I don't need a tutor.
Guitar is chilling it,
Kickboxing is killing it.
My mind races like Sonic,
I am iconic.

Nathan Moore (10)

Pretty Personality

A kennings poem

Magic maker
Slow writer
Quick thinker
Joke creator
Hyper runner
Make believer
Happy dreamer
Smart reader
Humble leader
Scared climber
Pony rider
Food lover
Sneaky walker
Crafty coder
Sensitive smeller.

Tanvi Saraswathi (8)

All About Spring Coming

Spring, spring, come on home
I want to see you, oh, oh, oh
Spring, spring, come
I want to see the flowers in my home
Spring, spring, I don't know how much fun
I will have with you
Spring, spring, oh, oh, oh
I love spring, hello.

Hiba Ahmed (6)

Samuel

S uper smart and handsome
A frican roots in me and an aspiring leader
M ultitalented with great understanding for the voiceless
U seful and bright
E xample of kindness
L oyal at all times.

Samuel Menakaya (10)

What Emotion Am I?

I make you laugh,
I make you smile,
I make you squeal,
I make you forget about bad things.
Now you're laughing, smiling and squealing the question is...
What emotion am I?

Answer: Silly.

Brandon Ford (10)

Who Am I Thinking Of?

There!
Fun, smart and messy,
Obviously kind and happy.

They love a splash of paint,
Always bold and fearless,
With a smile on their face.

Why would it not be?
It is *you!*

Isabella Ritson (8)

The Recipe Of Me!

J ugfuls of hugs
E ndless cups of kindness
S poonfuls of love
S prinkled with sass
I nfinite caring
C ombined with uniqueness
A dded together makes me!

Jessica Shaw (8)

All About Me: Chloe

C reative and love arts
H appy and cheerful child
L ikes many sports and has many hobbies
O range is the favourite colour and
E very fruit is my favourite food!

Chloe Lam (10)

This Is Me

F amily and friends are important to me
U sually make people laugh
N ever full up, always hungry
N ice looking, beautiful
Y ikes! What if there were two of me?

Alice Walton

My Cats' Lives

I've got one hundred cats,
I sustain them all to make them fat,
After that, I'll reward them with a tap,
Then I'll dump them in a trap,
After that, they'll look like a rat.

Riley Randles

This Is Me

I am intelligent,
But not extremely elegant.
My brain is filled with maths,
And I love having a bath.
I am passionate about school work,
Though have never been to New York.

Emily S (9)

Growing Up

I will change.
I will transform.
I will be different.
But change is a door.
And to not be daunted is the key.
Who knows what is waiting out there.
But at least there's you and me.

Isobel Tombs (9)

Madison

M e, myself and I
A mazing friend
D rama queen
I ntelligent
S uperstar
O bservant
N utty.

Madison Sullivan (9)

This Is Aania!

A ania loves art,
A nd a strawberry tart.
N ature walk
I s something she doesn't like,
A nd she really enjoys riding a bike.

Aania Bhamji (8)

My Best Dream
A haiku

Cricket match. Last ball.
I run in. Batsman sweating.
Stumps flying. Howzat?!

Benedict Swift (9)

Young Writers

YOUNG WRITERS INFORMATION

We hope you have enjoyed reading this book – and that you will continue to in the coming years.

If you're the parent or family member of an enthusiastic poet or story writer, do visit our website www.youngwriters.co.uk/subscribe and sign up to receive news, competitions, writing challenges and tips, activities and much, much more! There's lots to keep budding writers motivated!

If you would like to order further copies of this book, or any of our other titles, then please give us a call or order via your online account.

Young Writers
Remus House
Coltsfoot Drive
Peterborough
PE2 9BF
(01733) 890066
info@youngwriters.co.uk

Join in the conversation!
Tips, news, giveaways and much more!

f YoungWritersUK **✕** YoungWritersCW **◉** youngwriterscw